Designing Block Quilts

DESIGN & CREATE YOUR OWN PIXELATED QUILT PATTERNS

Quiltoni
SUPERPOWERED QUILTS!

Toni Smith

Designing Block Quilts
Toni Smith

Designing Block Quilts
Toni Smith
April 2018
Published by Quiltoni
PO Box 4763 Crofton, MD 21114 United States
© 2018 by Quiltoni
Art Director: Alex "Twill Distilled" Bellofatto
Editor: Rachel Neff
ISBN 978-1-7322295-0-1
LCCN

Table of Contents

Designing Block Quilts

Chapter One - The Math of Design

Math is one of the main backbones of quilting, but it's not always easy to figure out those pesky equations. Before you can understand the basics of designing a pixel quilt pattern, you need to understand how to get the size quilt you want. We will use a free pattern I offer as a guide to the concepts you will encounter throughout this book:

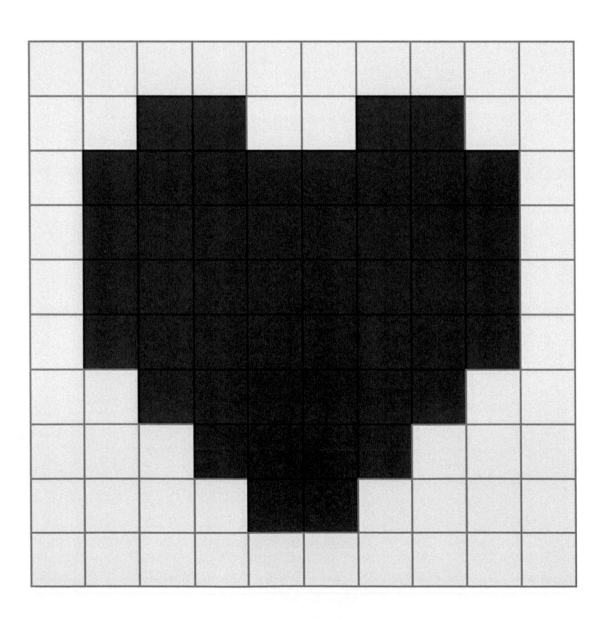

Calculating Size from Existing Sprites

If you have a design all ready to go from cross stitch, an existing sprite, or a previously made pattern, you can decide the size of the finished piece by deciding what size blocks you would like. For example, if we use the heart example, we have a 10x10 grid. While this example is with a square, this process will work for a rectangular-shaped quilt as well.

Formula =

Size of finished block multiplied by the number of blocks wide =
Finished Size of Width

Size of finished block multiplied by the number of blocks tall =
Finished Size of Length

0.75" blocks = 0.75" x 10" width = 7.5" Width
0.75" x 10" length = 7.5" Length

1" blocks = 1" x 10" = 10" x 10"

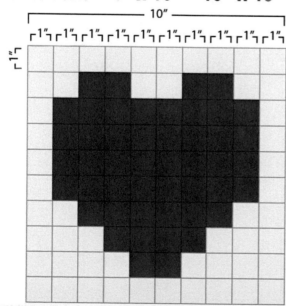

2.5" blocks = 2.5" x 10" = 25" x 25"

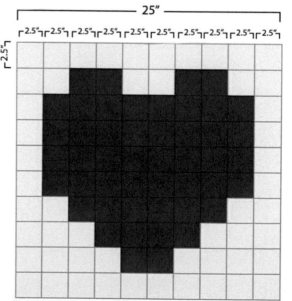

Calculating Size from Existing Sprites

Those dimensions are for the finished blocks once they are sewn into the quilt top. In order to have that finished size, add in a ¼" seam so we know how big to cut our initial fabric pieces. Remember to add this seam allowance to each side of the block, which is left, right, top, and bottom. So, this means you will add a total of ½" to each block. The 0.75" finished blocks would be created from fabric that is originally 1.25" cut blocks.

1" block = Cut 1.5"   2.5" block = Cut 3"

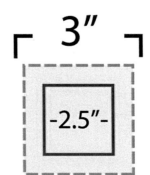

┌ 1.5" ┐   ┌ 3" ┐

-1"-   -2.5"-

Let's try the formula using a quilt top that is 20 blocks wide by 35 blocks long.

0.75" blocks =	1" blocks =	2.5" blocks =
0.75" x 20" = 15" width	1" x 20" = 20" width	2.5" x 20" = 50" width
0.75" x 35" = 26.25" length	1" x 35" = 35" length	2.5" x 35" = 87.5" length
Cut Blocks 1.25"	Cut Blocks 1.5"	Cut Blocks 3"

Calculating Size of Pattern Based on Finished Quilt Size

Formula =

**Finished size of width divided by finished size of block =
number of blocks wide**

**Finished size of length divided by finished size of block =
number of blocks long**

**Start with the assumption that you know the size of the quilt you want to make
and you need to figure out how much space you have to design your sprite.**

**If we decide to have a quilt measure 20" by 20", divide the width and length by the finished
size of each block. A finished size of 2" squares would give us 10 blocks for
width and for length (20/2 = 10). Then add the ½" for seam allowance. Cut 2.5" blocks.**

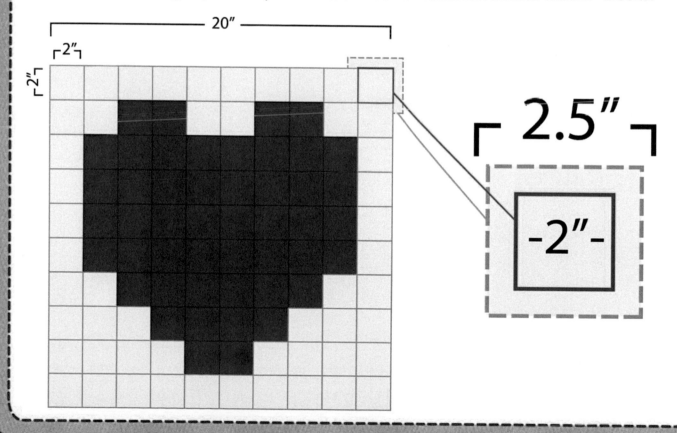

Calculating Size of Pattern Based on Finished Quilt Size

IT'S TIME FOR "TONI TIPS!"

YOU MAY WANT TO PICK NICE ROUND NUMBERS THAT WILL DIVIDE EVENLY INTO THE SIZE OF YOUR QUILT.

1" blocks (cut 1.5") =
(20/1) = 20 blocks by 20 blocks

5" blocks (cut 5.5") =
(20/5) = 4 blocks by 4 blocks

Using 2" blocks you would have a space of 600 blocks to design your sprite (20x30 space):

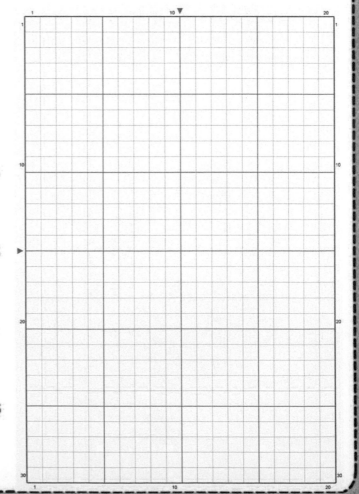

Try it with a quilt that will be:
40" wide by 60" long.

1" blocks (cut 1.5") =
(40/1) by (60/1) = 40 blocks by 60 blocks

4" blocks (cut 4.5") =
(40/4) by (60/4) = 10 blocks by 15 blocks

5" blocks (cut 5.5") =
(40/5) by (60/5) = 8 blocks by 12 blocks

2" blocks (cut 2.5") =
(40/2) by (60/2) = 20 blocks by 30 blocks

But What If I Want Borders?

There are two options to account for borders when deciding the size of your canvas

Option 1

Deduct the size of the borders from the canvas size.

For example, if we were working with the previous example (20 by 30 blocks using a 2" finished block) and we wanted one 4" finished border, we would deduct 4 blocks from the width and 4 blocks from the length. This is because you have 2 blocks that "frame" the quilt.

So there are 2 blocks on the left, right, top, and bottom.

That would now give us a canvas size of 16 by 26 to work with when creating the design sprite.

(20 original blocks - 4 border blocks)
by
(30 original blocks - 4 border blocks).

BORDER

DESIGN AREA
CANVAS SIZE
16 x 26

But What If I Want Borders?

There are two options to account for borders when deciding the size of your canvas

Option 2
Draw it in the design

When accounting for the borders, draw them right on the canvas and account for it in the pattern.

This also allows you to choose which colors for the border would complement your sprite.

IT'S TIME FOR "TONI TIPS!"

THIS IS THE EASIER OPTION AND THE ONE I USE!

BORDER

DESIGN AREA
CANVAS SIZE
10 x 10

But What If I Want Borders?

If we look at the heart again and want to make it larger to add a border, we extend the pixels and try different colors to see which color we like better.

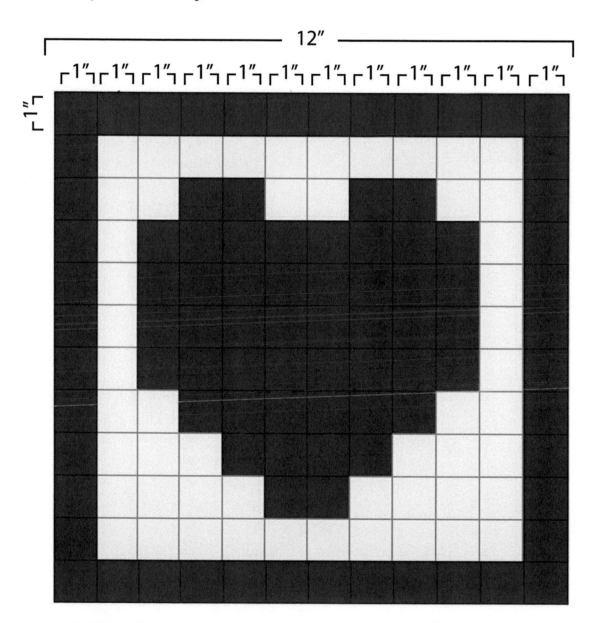

Instead of a 10x10 space, we now have a 12x12 space.
Even though the finished border is only 1 pixel wide,
2 pixels total were added to the length and 2 to the width.

Chapter Two - Designing Your Sprite

Hire a Spriter

There are people who specialize in original sprite design such as Geek Mythology Crafts. For a small fee, they can design a sprite for you and you can go right to turning your sprite into a pattern. When commissioning your pixel art, be sure to communicate the following best practice design guidelines to the artist: limit the color palette, use contrasting colors, and outline where necessary. Also inform your designer that you'll be using the design in a quilt project, and work out any agreements for future use of the design.

Graph Paper

Using graph paper to make your designs is inexpensive and easy. You only need to secure graph paper with the same number of squares that match the size of your design area or "frame" for your working area. For example, if we decided to work with the 20x30 design from the last chapter, we would need a 20x30 space within our graph paper. Most graph paper in the size you will need is available at retail locations or online.

MagnaBitz

MagnaBitz are tiny magnetic-backed colored tiles used to create and recreate pixelated images. It's like having colored graph paper that can be changed. This is the preferred method of designing for those who enjoy designing on graph paper, but who also want to move the colors around to see how the design looks in different ways.

Check out the graph paper on Pg 32 that will fit with your MagnaBitz!

LET'S GET PIXELATED!

Cross Stitch Software

There are many options for cross stitch software on the market. My preferred one is KG Chart by Iktsoft, which runs on computers and has a stitch sketch app for Apple devices. Using software allows you to change your design as you are creating it, which you can't do with graph paper.

You can use a large color palette to not only fill in colors, but also change colors. Changing colors is helpful because it can let you explore the background to see how it might look. The heart square from Chapter 1 was created using KG Chart. I was able to see how the heart looked using different colors for the background before I settled on cream. But, to show you the versatility of the program, here are a few of the other background colors.

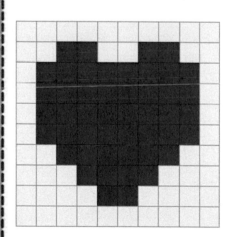 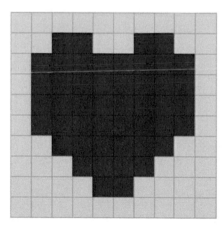 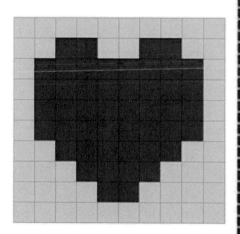

You can also import a photo or other image into the software and adjust it to meet your needs.

Things to Keep in Mind Before You Design

Before we can start figuring out our actual design, there are a few things you need to keep in mind: number of colors, fabric contrast, outlines, design, inspiration, and modification.

Number of Colors

The more colors you have in a sprite, the more detailed and shadowed the final image may appear. The same is not true for pixel quilts. The more colors you include in the design, the more complicated it becomes to quilt. In part, this is due to the nature of quilting. The more colors you choose, the more nuances you have to keep track of when sewing your final quilt top. Also, you may run into difficulties finding fabric in all the shades you want. Simple is better. Instead of having three shades of the same sort of red, pick one.

Fabric Contrast

Keep in mind the color of fabrics you may want to use when designing your quilt. If you have a tan color next to a yellow color, are they different enough so they won't get lost and blend together? Make sure to have contrast between your colors to have your entire design stand out. Here is a quilt I made in the early years of my quilting before I understood contrast. Notice how the skin tone in the face and arms blends into the background. Today, I would choose a different shade or a different background color to ensure there was enough contrast to have the sprite's face stand out.

Things to Keep in Mind Before You Design

Outlines

One of the ways you can create a good contrast between the background and your sprite is by outlining the sprite. You do not need to add a thick outline, just a basic color that surrounds your sprite. For example, when I designed the sprite to the right for Real Life Comics, I knew I wanted to use a lot of browns. To make sure there was a division between the background and the sprite, I used black outlining to make it pop.

Inspiration

Deciding on a subject matter for your project can be tricky, but there are tons of resources to take inspiration from. If you have a particular character, object or theme in mind, you can use an existing sprite from a video game.

IF YOU ARE CREATING A PATTERN FOR MORE THAN YOUR OWN PERSONAL USE, CONSULT A LAWYER ABOUT THE INTRICACIES OF COPYRIGHT LAW.

The Spriters Resource (https://www.spriters-resource.com/) is an amazing website that will often have what you're looking for. The sprites are laid out on sheets with transparent or flat-colored backgrounds so they will be easy to extract and edit for your quilt pattern.

You can also do a quick Google search or web search with keywords such as "pixel art" or "sprite" along with your desired subject matter to find a plethora of pixel art examples.

However, when sourcing your sprite design in these ways, always be sure to acquire permission from the original designer. In the case of sprites directly from video games, you'll want to modify them to make them workable for your quilt pattern.

Things to Keep in Mind Before You Design

Modification

There is a vast selection of image editing software that can be used for sprite design, many of which are free of charge. Here are a few recommendations:

Graphics Gale (https://graphicsgale.com/us/)   **Paint.net** (https://www.getpaint.net/)

GIMP (https://www.gimp.org/)   **Piskel** (https://www.piskelapp.com/)

Piskel is a great way to start out designing your own sprite, or even editing an existing one to suit your pattern needs. It has simple drawing tools and a grid so you can paint your image pixel by pixel and choose from the entire spectrum of colors to work with.

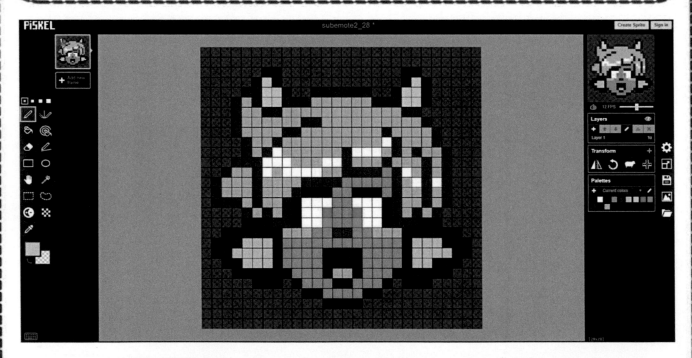

You can import an existing sprite easily with a few clicks and get right to work on editing the colors and outline as necessary for your quilt pattern. When you're finished designing, you can save it to work on later in the app, or you can save it to your computer as a PNG file to print or use while you're designing your quilt.
Studying existing pixel art is a great way to learn how to draw it yourself. Find examples of styles and designs that you like and pay attention to the way the pixels are placed.
You'll be drawing your own pixelated masterpieces in no time!
Now that you have your very own sprite design, you're on your way to creating an amazing quilt!

Three Different Methods

Now that you have your design, it is time to create a pattern.

There are three different methods you can choose from to pattern your newly created sprite:
1 Pixel = 1 Block, The Quiltoni Way, or Stripping.

For each method, nest your seams. This is when you iron your seams in opposite directions so they line up and allow the fabric to line up perfectly for perfect points.

Notice how the bottom row has the seams ironed to the left and the row above it has the rows ironed to the right.

Once your seams have been ironed and layed out, combine your pieces or rows by lining up each seam in opposite directions and pin them in place.

Notice how the opposite seams line up to have a perfect point.

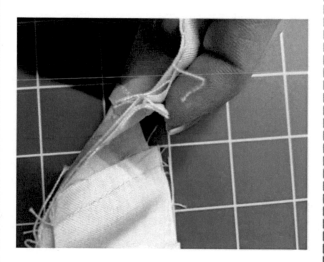

Sew your row or combined pieces.

Three Different Methods

1 Pixel = 1 Block

This is the traditional method of making pixel quilts. Your quilt looks more like an actual sprite and each block is separated. This method is explained in detail in Chapter 4.

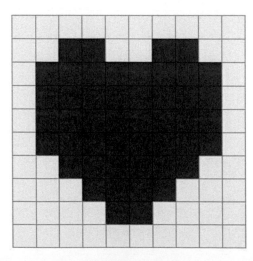

The downside to this method is the time it takes. It is the longest way to create your pattern.

Three Different Methods

The Quiltoni Way

This is the method I use to create all of my patterns. The quilt you create takes a fraction of the time compared to the the 1 Pixel = 1 Block method. You are able to make quilts more quickly than other methods.

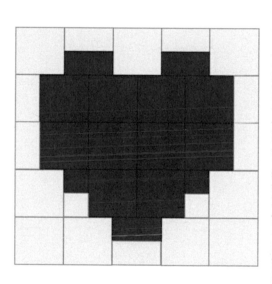

There are two drawbacks to this method though.

First, the pattern itself takes longer to make.

Second, the quilt itself does not have the complete pixelated look as the 1 Pixel = 1 Block method.

This method is explained in detail in Chapter 5.

Three Different Methods

Stripping

This is a hybrid of the previous two methods.

Look at each line of your quilt and combine
all of the same color blocks that
are touching in a row. For example,
if you were creating the heart block with this
method your pattern would look like this:

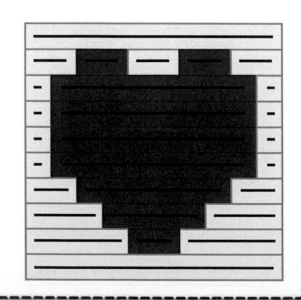

Three Different Methods

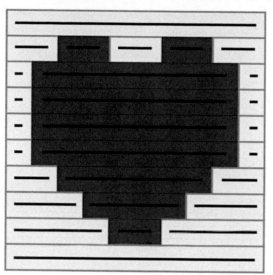

If you wanted 1.5" finished blocks you would assume a height of 2".

Multiply the number of blocks in each strip times the finished block size of 1.5" plus the seam allowance of ½".
10 blocks across - 10" x 1.5" + 0.5" = 15.5"
8 blocks across - 8" x 1.5" + 0.5" = 12.5"
6 blocks across - 6" x 1.5" + 0.5" = 9.5"
4 Blocks across - 4" x 1.5" + 0.5" = 6.5"
3 Blocks across - 3" x 1.5" + 0.5" = 5"
2 Blocks across - 2" x 1.5" + 0.5" = 3.5"
1 Block across - 1" x 1.5" + 0.5" = 2"

Once you know your measurements, count how many of each piece you need.

Cream:

(2) 15.5" x 2"
(10 blocks x 1.5" plus seam allowance of 0.5")

(2) 6.5" x 2"

(2) 5" x 2"

(5) 3.5" x 2"

(8) 2" x 2"

15.5" x 2"		
3.5" x 2"	3.5" x 2"	3.5" x 2"
2"x 2"		2"x 2"
2"x 2"		2"x 2"
2"x 2"		2"x 2"
2"x 2"		2"x 2"
3.5" x 2"		3.5" x 2"
- 5" x 2" -		- 5" x 2" -
– 6.5" x 2" –		– 6.5" x 2" –
15.5" x 2"		

Now let's calculate how many strips to cut. Multiply each quantity by the length of the strip that needs to be cut and divide by 40 (the width of standard fabric is 42 inches, so we round down to the nearest 10).
(15.5x2 + 6.5x2 + 5x2 + 3.5x5 + 2x8) / 40 = (31 + 13 + 10 + 17.5 + 16) / 40 = 86.9 / 40 = 2.17
Round up to the nearest whole number. So we cut 3 strips of 2" wide cream fabric.

Three Different Methods

red:

(4) 12.5" x 2"
(8 blocks x 1.5 plus seam allowance of 0.5")

(1) 9.5" x 2"

(1) 6.5" x 2"

(3) 3.5" x 2"

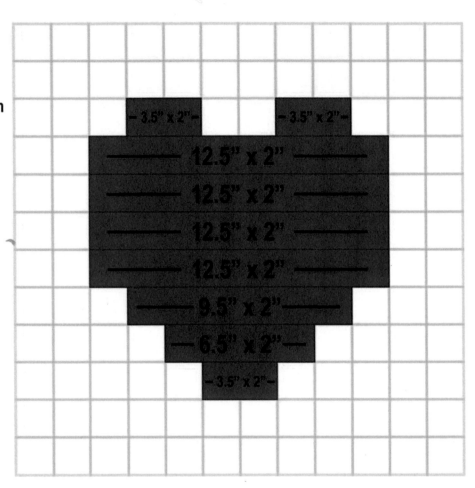

(12.5x4 + 9.5x1 + 6.5x1 + 3.5x3) / 40 = (50 + 9.5 + 6.5 + 10.5) / 40 = 76.5 / 40 = 1.91
Round up to the nearest whole number. So we cut 2 strips of 2" wide Red fabric.

Cut each of the pieces out of the strips.

Lay the pieces of each row out, sew, and iron seams in opposite directions for easy nesting.
Sew the rows together.
Your quilt top is complete!

Traditional Method

This is the traditional method of making pixel quilts. Your quilt looks more like an actual sprite and each block is separated. It is also a great method to use up your scrap stash.

Cutting each block out

This is exactly what you think it is. Cut each block to the size you determined (including the seam allowance). The benefit to using a cross stitch program with this method is that the program tells you exactly how many blocks to cut out. Because you are creating one square for each pixel, doing a 1 Pixel = 1 Block method takes the most time to design and complete.

Traditional Method

Once you count how many blocks of each color you have, write it down (or print it out from the cross stitch program). Let's look at the Heart as a 1 Pixel = 1 Block design.

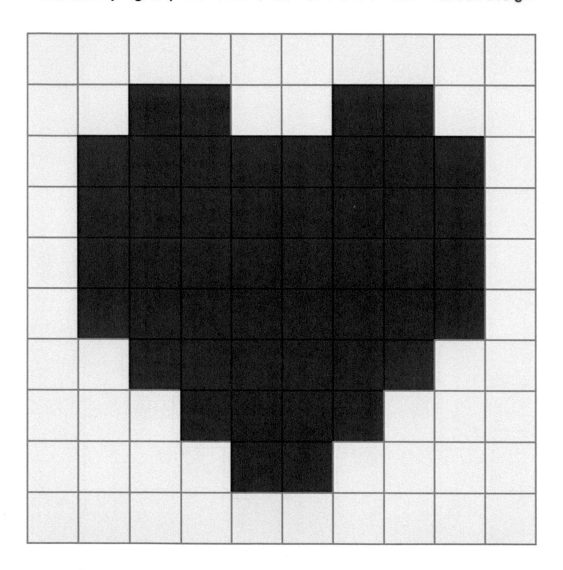

In this design, we have 52 cream-colored pieces and 48 red pieces.
We decided our finished blocks will be 1.5". So we cut blocks 2" x 2".

Once all of the pieces have been cut out lay them out, row by row. Sew and iron the seams of the rows in opposite directions. (See the beginning of Chapter 3 for directions on how to nest seams).

Sew the rows together.

Fusible Interfacing

With this method, you use a grid of fusible interfacing to speed up the process of 1 Pixel= 1 Block. Blocks are cut out and ironed to the interfacing. Another plus to this method is there are no pins and is easier for young children to learn to sew.

The downside to this method is the top is a little stiffer because you are adding another layer to the quilt. Even though it is faster than the 1 Pixel= 1 Block method, it is still slower than the Quiltoni Way and the Stripping method of making a pixel quilt.

First, find a fusible gridded interfacing the size of your cut blocks. The heart block uses a 2" gridded fusible interfacing for the example which complements 1.5" finished blocks.

Cut each block out just like in the previous example. We will use the heart again and cut out 52 cream-colored pieces and 48 red pieces. Cut your fusible interfacing the size of your finished project. If it is larger than your interfacing, create it in separate sections and sew the finished sections together.

Lay out the interfacing with the rough side facing up. Lay two rows of your design onto the corresponding blocks with the right side of the fabric facing up. Iron the fabric onto the interfacing with NO steam.

BE CAREFUL NOT TO TOUCH THE UNCOVERED INTERFACING WITH YOUR IRON BECAUSE THE INTERFACING MAY STICK TO THE IRON PLATE AND BE DIFFICULT, IF NOT IMPOSSIBLE, TO REMOVE

Fusible Interfacing

Fold the rows toward each other so the right sides are pressed against each other.

Sew a ¼" inch seam along the edge the folded part creates.

Add rows one at a time, ironing and sewing them as you add them.

Once all rows are added to the fusible interfacing and sewn, iron all of the rows in one direction on the wrong or back side. You may use the steam setting on your iron. Turn your project over and iron on the correct or right side of the quilt top.

Separate each of the seams you just sewed. With lightweight interfacing, this is done by ripping the interfacing. With medium interfacing, cut the interfacing very carefully to avoid cutting the fabric ironed to the top of the quilt.

Fold the far right column over the column to the immediate row on the left, right sides together. Finger press the rows.

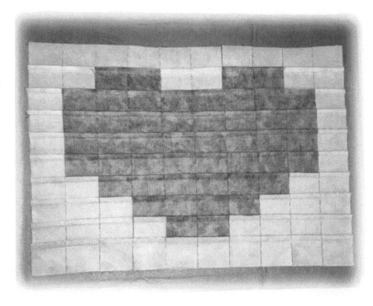

Fusible Interfacing

Finger press the seams in opposite directions, nesting them as you sew them. Repeat for each of the columns.

Iron all of the columns in one direction on the wrong or back side. It is ok to use steam at this point. Turn your project over and iron on the correct or right side. Your quilt top is complete!

Maximizing Efficiency!

Sometimes efficiency in quilting is just as important as the pattern. Some people don't have a lot of time or need to keep their attention focused to finish a quilt. The Quiltoni Way maximizes efficiency in quilting. You are able to create a lap-sized top in as little as one day.

Instead of cutting the individual blocks, you create strips to combine together. Separate your design into rows that are 2 pixels tall. Let's look at the heart block with this done.

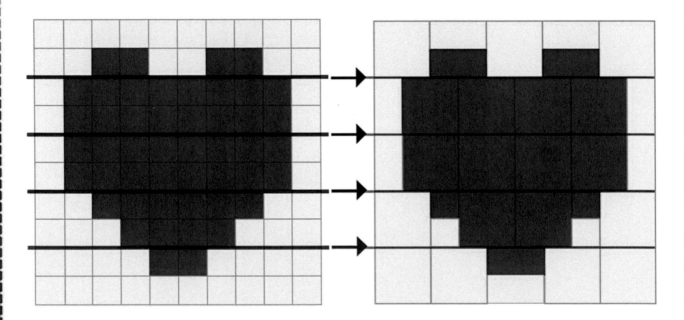

There are three different sizes of blocks that you will use.

You are also combining colors together using the smaller two sizes.

Take these pieces and fit them into your design.

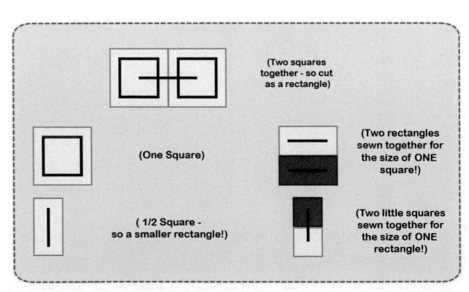

(Two squares together - so cut as a rectangle)

(One Square)

(Two rectangles sewn together for the size of ONE square!)

(1/2 Square - so a smaller rectangle!)

(Two little squares sewn together for the size of ONE rectangle!)

Maximizing Efficiency!

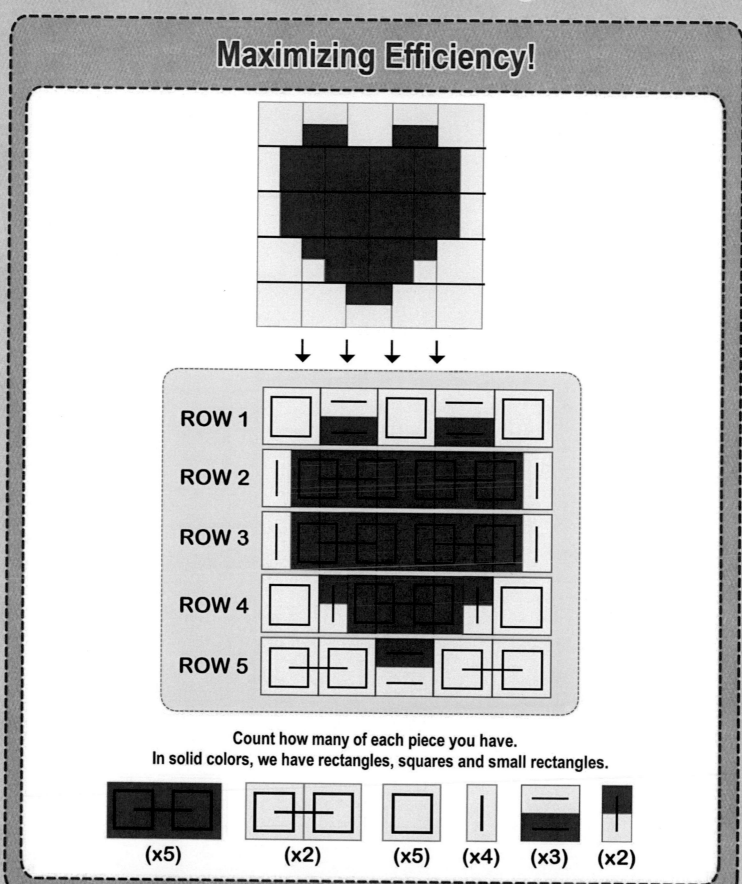

ROW 1

ROW 2

ROW 3

ROW 4

ROW 5

Count how many of each piece you have.
In solid colors, we have rectangles, squares and small rectangles.

(x5)   (x2)   (x5)   (x4)   (x3)   (x2)

Maximizing Efficiency!

The formulas to find each width would be:

Finished Block Size x 4 + ½" = Width of Rectangle

Finished Block Size x 2 + ½" = Width of Square

Finished Block Size + ½" = Width of Small Rectangle

Rectangle : 1 ½" x 4 + ½" = 6 ½"

Square : 1 ½" x 2 + ½" = 3 ½"

Small Rectangle : 1 ½" + ½" = 2"

In order to determine the number of strips to cut, multiply the width of the piece by how many of those pieces you need.

Then add those numbers together and divide by 40 (the width of standard fabric is 42 inches, so we round down to the nearest 10) and round the number up to the next whole number.

[(Width Rectangle x # Rectangles) + (Width Square x # Squares) + (Width Small Rectangle x # Small Rectangles)] / 40

Maximizing Efficiency!

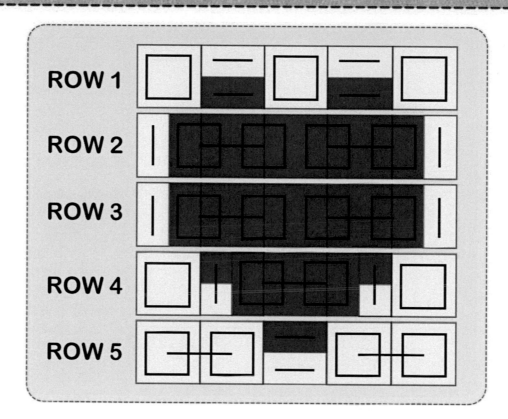

ROW 1
ROW 2
ROW 3
ROW 4
ROW 5

Cream

2 Rectangles
5 Squares
4 Small Rectangles
[(6 ½" x 2) + (3 ½" x 5)] + (2" x 4) / 40
13" + 17 ½" + 8" = 38 ½"/ 40
In this case we get 0.9625,
rounded up would be 1 strip.

Red

5 Rectangles
(6 ½" x 5) /40
32 ½" / 40 = 0.8125,
rounded up would be 1 strip.

Then figure out the size of the strips based on the size of your finished design.
Start with the size of your finished squares. Don't forget seam allowance.
Finished block size x 2 + ½" seam allowance = size of single colored strips.
Our finished squares in this case are 1 ½".
1 ½" x 2 + ½" = 3 ½" strips

Maximizing Efficiency!

Now let's look at the combined pieces.

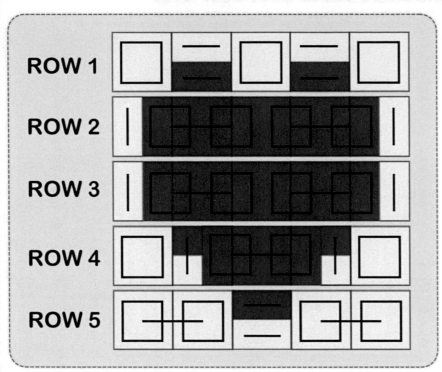

(x3)   (x2)

(The widths would be the same as the Square and Small Rectangle.)

Finished Block Size x 2 + ½" = Width of Combined Square
Finished Block Size + ½" = Width of Combined Small Rectangle
Combined Square - 1 ½" x 2 + ½" = 3 ½"
Combined Small Rectangle - 1 ½" + ½" = 2"

In order to determine the number of strips to cut, use the same formula as the solid colors, but remember it is the same number of strips for each color you combine.
[(Width Combined Square x # Squares) + (Width Combined Small Rectangle x # Small Rectangles)] / 40
[(3 ½ x 3) + (2 x 2) /40
10 ½ + 4 = 14 ½ / 40 = 0.3625 rounded up to 1.

We would cut 1 strip of Red and 1 strip of Cream to sew together.

To figure out the size of the combined strips just take your finished square size plus seam allowance (it is also the width of the small rectangle). 1 ½" + ½" = 2" inch strips.

Maximizing Efficiency!

Now that your math is complete, I find it easier to create a grid of all of the strips you need to cut.

COLOR	3 ½" STRIP	2" STRIP
■ RED	1	1
□ CREAM	1	1

Then create your quilt.

Cut your 3 ½" strips first. With the 3 ½" strips:

From the Red fabric cut :
→ (x5) 3 ½" x 6 ½" rectangles   (x5)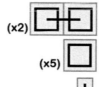

From the Cream fabric cut :
→ (x2) 3 ½" x 6 ½" rectangles   (x2)
→ (x5) 3 ½" x 3 ½" square   (x5)
→ (x4) 2" x 3 ½" rectangle   (x4)

Sew your 2 inch combined strips, right sides together. Cut your strips in half.
Take your cut seams and nest the seams (lining the seams up in opposite directions to allow the fabric to line up perfectly) by laying one right side up and the other one wrong side up on top of it.
Line up your strips evenly and trim the edge.

TOP VIEW:

SIDE VIEW:

Maximizing Efficiency!

Then cut the remainding pieces:
→ (x2) 3 ½" x 3½" squares (4 Total)
→ (x1) 3 ½" x 2" rectangles (2 Total)

Now it is time to lay out all of the pieces. Start with the first row and lay each piece right side up, making sure you pay attention to the direction the seam is facing.

Always make sure the seam is facing the direction of the arrow. If the seam is facing up or down, make sure that the piece next to it is nested (has the seam in the opposite direction). Re-iron any seams that need to be changed to a different direction.

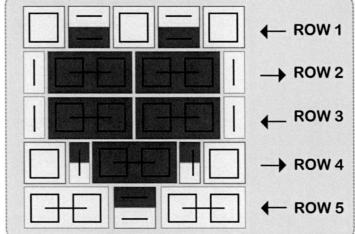

Assemble each row, sewing right sides together and seams facing the direction of the arrow.

Finally, sew the rows together. It does not matter which direction your seams face when sewing this step.

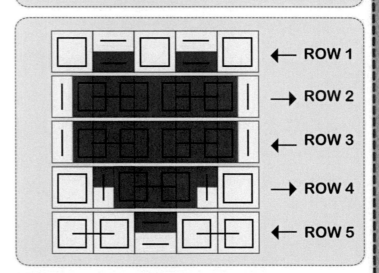

Add any additional borders as you wish!

To add borders, measure the length of the quilt and cut strips of fabric in the width you want your border to be.
Sew the strips along the left and right of the quilt. Iron seams away from the quit top and trim the edges.
Measure the width of the quilt and cut strips of fabric in the same width as the borders on the left and right. Sew the strips along the top and bottom of the quilt. Iron seams away from the quilt and trim the edges.

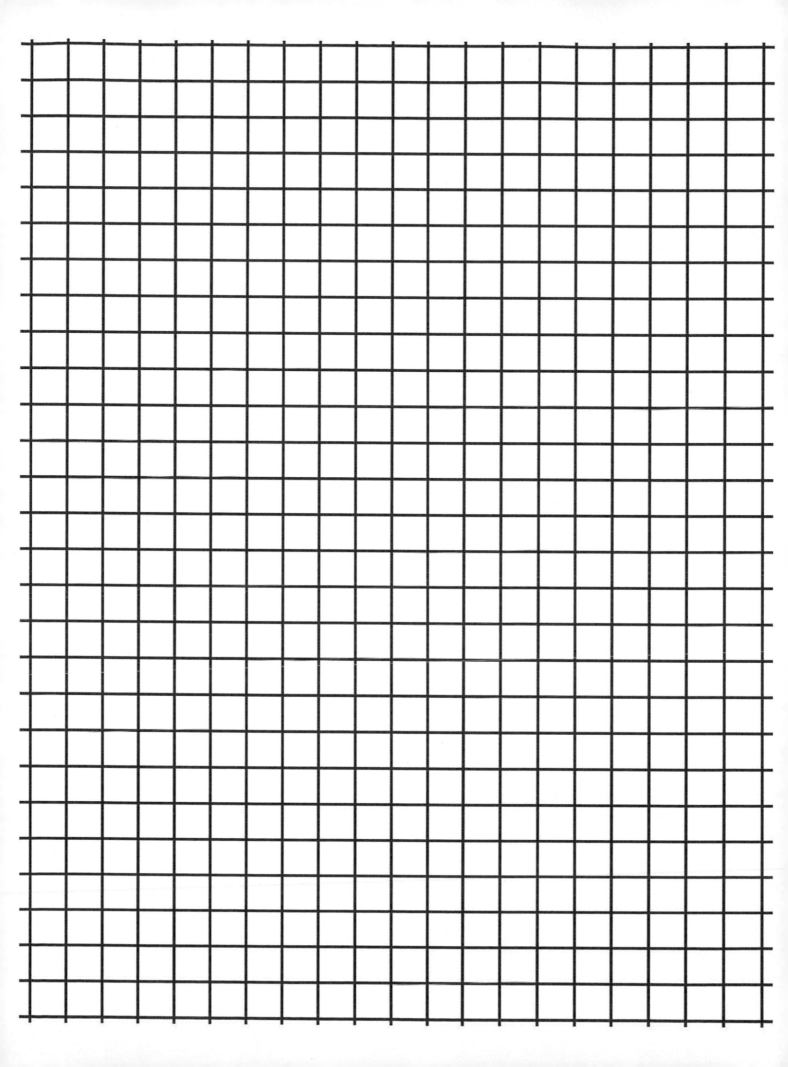

Resources

Free Graph Paper - http://www.printfreegraphpaper.com/

MagaBitz - https://www.magnabitz.com/

KG Chart by IKTsoft - https://www.iktsoft.net/kgchart-en/kgchart/

Spriter's Resource - https://www.spriters-resource.com/

Graphics Gale - https://graphicsgale.com/us/

Paint.net - https://www.getpaint.net/

Gimp - https://www.gimp.org

Piskel - https://www.piskelapp.com/

Glossary

Seam Allowance - The area between the edge of the fabric and the stitched line. All seam allowances in this book are ¼".

Finished Size - The size your piece of fabric or quilt will be after it is completely sewn together.

Canvas Size - The area you are working with when designing your pattern.

Borders - The area around your design that frames your quilt.

Sprite - A pixelated image.

Spriter - A person who specializes in creating original sprites.

Nesting Seams - Ironing seams in opposite directions so they line up and allow the fabric to be sewn together with perfect points.

Fusible Interfacing - Interfacing that has glue on one side of the material. For this book, we use gridded fusible interfacing that has a printed grid on the glue side that washes away.

Toni has been selling her original comic book and video game quilts at conventions for years. Her pattern line of pixelated quilts teach the basics of quilting, while teaching experienced quilters new techniques. She also travels to teach classes, lecture, and give trunk shows.

Now you can create your own pixel quilts. Learn the basics of pixel quilt design and patterning to create your very own designs!

Made in the USA
San Bernardino, CA
01 May 2018